A MODERN GUIDE TO SOCIAL MEDIA ETIQUETTE

MAX MCPHERSON

Printed in the United States of America

First Printing, 2018

ISBN 978-0-9876360-0-3 Paperback
ISBN 978-0-9876360-1-0 Ebook

www.max-mcpherson.com

Introduction

What is Social Media?

Social media refers to web-based or digital technology platforms that promote the sharing of information or facilitate communication, either with friends, fans, or other online communities. The content posted on such platforms tends to be user-generated or contextually relevant. Social media platforms emerged in the 1990s, initially in the form of basic and selective online forums, but launched into the mainstream with Classmates, LinkedIn, and MySpace in the early 2000s. The social media landscape then exploded around 2007 with the rapid and global adoption of Facebook and has continued to expand ever since.

Facebook now reports over a third of the global population uses its social media platform each month, and as it has grown, the company has added other brands, like Instagram, Messenger, and WhatsApp, to its portfolio of services. Other popular social media platforms include YouTube, Twitter, Tumbler, WeChat, Snapchat, Pinterest, Weibo, and the Chinese site Baidu Tieba.

Most people now have at least one social media profile, which has led to a whole new set of rules for engaging in the social media world. This guide outlines some key principles for navigating within this landscape to get the best out of your social media experience.

1. Always remember that anything you post on a profile or wall is public. So, don't post unless you want all your friends and their friends to see it. This is especially important for private matters. If you need to talk directly to a person, send a personal message, through, e.g., Messenger, WhatsApp, or call/SMS them. Birthday messages are pretty much the only messages that are usually completely safe to post to someone's wall.

When uploading a photo or video, check that everyone (not just yourself!) looks good in it. It is just common courtesy to ensure everyone looks their best, as no one is going to thank you for posting a photo they were not prepared for. This is especially relevant if you want to "Tag" your friends in the post. And remember, only tag people who actually feature in the photo or video!

2. When uploading photos, be sure to limit the number uploaded at any one time. Choose the best ones only, and feel free to do some light touch-ups using your photo editor if necessary. A good rule of thumb is to limit uploads to no more than 10 photos in a single post.

3. Other than photos of your own children or grandchildren, avoid posting or uploading photos of anyone else's family members (group shots should be fine). Some people don't want pictures of their children on social media, as they could find it a violation of privacy.

4. It's good to have your own opinions, and social media is a great place to share them with a wide audience. But note, not everyone may agree with you, and some may even completely disagree. Healthy debate allows different points of view to be heard; however, know where your "line" is, and at what point you are willing to walk away to keep the peace.

5. The two topics that are often the most sensitive to discuss with friends and family are religion and politics. This is also true for discussions on social media. There could be relevant or applicable moments to do so, but tread ever so carefully to avoid offending anyone.

6. Only use your status updates or check-ins to announce relevant and newsworthy information. No one wants to know about your routine daily chores. Share something that your social media friends would find interesting or amusing.

7. Do not under any circumstances post a photo or check-in if you know any friends will be annoyed or upset that they haven't been invited to an event. This can cause real issues between friends, both on social media and in the real world.

8. Don't ruin anyone's announcements (pregnancy, engagement, new house or job, etc.) by sharing information on social media before they have. This is particularly relevant for weddings; it is, however, safe to post after the bride or groom have posted content themselves.

9. Avoid referring to something a person has done on social media in real life. If you do, you could cause that person to feel uncomfortable, so unless they bring it up, best not to mention it.

10. Post comments thoughtfully on social media. By all means make comments, but refrain from commenting on every post from a single person, or on every post you see that day. It can come across as slightly creepy! This is especially true for your own direct family. Applying the "1 out of 5" rule can help; this means limiting your posts to 1 comment for every 5 posts a person makes. Also, when making a comment, try to keep it relevant to that person's original post.

11. The "Like" button on many social media platforms has evolved over time and now often includes multiple options that relate to particular emotions (happy, sad, confused, etc.). Be sure to use the correct one when reacting to a post. Again, don't "Like" every post a person makes, and don't just like every post you see— try to be more selective.

12. If you are searching through someone's profile, in particular their photos, be careful not to "Like" or comment on their old ones. The person will receive a notification, and if the photo or event is really old, they might wonder why you are trawling through their profile.

13.

While social media platforms embrace a more informal form of communication, they are still communication vehicles. It's important to ensure correct spelling/grammar and punctuation. If you don't, be prepared for people to comment and possibly even criticize you. Shortened words and/or slang, e.g., YOLO, LOL, WTF, IRL, etc., can be appropriately used, but before posting make sure you understand their meaning.

14. Emojis or emoticons are great tools for adding tone, meaning, or empathy to social media posts, but be sure you understand the meaning behind the symbols. Also, try not to overuse them in one post. Some common examples are: 🍦🌙🎉🍾🧤🤟.

15. Hashtags (using the # symbol) can be short or long, but only use them if they have some relevance to your post.

16. CAPITAL letters in the digital world give the impression of yelling. Use these only in an appropriate context.

17. In posts or comments, try to minimize your own emotions, as these can be seen by a large audience. Avoid coming across as vague, secretive, enlisting pity, purposely "baiting," scolding, or arguing, and always limit any profanity. There might be times when doing so is acceptable, but assume these times will be rare.

18. A recent trend is to post on the wall of a company you have a grievance against. Although this usually means the company will react quickly (No business likes negative feedback!), understand that your post will be completely public, and all your friends will see it. Sometimes a private message to the business is just as effective—and much more discrete.

19. Be wary of chain posts on social media. These typically suggest you repost for good luck or to avoid some sort of superstition. Most of these might seem like they are for a good cause or charity, and indeed they may be, but too many of these posts in your feed can leave a negative impression on your social media followers. If you feel strongly about one of these, by all means post it, but try to be selective.

20. Don't feel you have to "Share" everything you see. The "Share" button helps project other stories or content into your own social media feed, but make sure you only share stories or content that your social media friends will want to read or see.

21. Don't make social media friend requests to people you don't know. This is especially true for friends of your direct family. Unless you have a personal relationship with someone in real life, it's probably best to leave them alone.

22. Never ever post a spoiler about a new TV show, movie, or book that you have watched or read. This will frustrate your friends on social media and could cause them to reprimand you.

23. Playing games on your phone is perfectly fine; just don't freely invite all your social media friends to join you—as it can become annoying to constantly receive invites to mobile games. Gaming apps are well-known for attempting to increase their usage by encouraging users to enlist their own friends to play (It's easy and cheap advertising). So, the best advice is to press the "Skip" button when asked to suggest the game to friends.

24. Never disclose any financial or personal details on social media. This includes your phone number, email and home address, as well as your bank account or credit card numbers. Digital fraud and scams are so prevalent now, and providing these details could allow someone to forge your identity.

25. While the increased use of social media has created new etiquette norms, it has also driven a much more connected world. The way we communicate has changed significantly, but at its essence, communication is still about sharing stories and ideas, celebrating milestones, and engaging with friends and family—now just instantaneously and on a much larger scale. On the flipside, because our communication is more public, there is an increased risk of offending people. Being aware of the pitfalls of social media use can help to minimize this risk and make social media communication a much more positive experience. So, be careful, but enjoy!